To Larry

Good Luck!

Bill Clinton

DISCOVER THE *NEW* TRUTH ABOUT WHAT IT TAKES

GETTING TO THE NEXT LEVEL

A Continuing Story of Entrepreneurship

Business, Race and Our
Common Goal to Be Competitive

Melvin J. Gravely II, Ph.D.

Edited by Shirley Allen
Cover design and inside layout by Ad Graphics, Inc.
Internal graphics designed by Amy Winegardner
Printed in the United States of America.

Gravely, II, Melvin J.,
Getting to the Next Level:
Business, Race and Our Common Goal to Be Competitive

ISBN-13: 978-0-9656194-9-3
ISBN-10: 0-9656194-9-4

Library of Congress Control Number: 2006939537

Mailing address:
Impact Group Publishers
P.O. Box 621170, Cincinnati, OH 45262-1170

OTHER BOOKS IN THE SERIES
BY MEL GRAVELY

When Black and White Make Green
The Next Evolution in Business & Race

The Lost Art of Entrepreneurship
Rediscovering the Principles That Will Guarantee Your Success

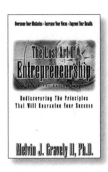

ACKNOWLEDGMENTS

This book represents months of research including many conversations with major organizations, communities and minority business owners. I am honored to work in significant ways with some of the brightest minds and best thinkers in the nation. You guys continue to overwhelm me with your talent and insight. Thank you.

To my wife Chandra. You are the ultimate partner and my constant support. You always encourage me to tackle the next challenge. I love you.

To the group of great friends and colleagues who invested many hours reviewing this book and providing valuable input. I am forever in your debt for your investment in me. Thank you all:

DeLynne Ano, Farad Ali, Angie Avery, Clifford Bailey, Emmett Drane, Mark Dulaney, Vanessa Freytag, Jewel Grafton, Ed Jackson, Arlene Koth, Brian Matthews, Joe Mudd, Bob Ontiveros, Lisa Switalski, Sandra Talley, Adrienne Trimble, Mike Washington, Icy Williams, and Otis Williams.

A special thank you to Robin Bischoff for everything you do everyday. It is always considerably more than you have to. You are the oil that makes it all run smoothly. Thank you.

TABLE OF CONTENTS

Introduction 6

Chapter 1   –   Am I Landing or Taking Off? 9

Chapter 2   –   There's a Role for Everyone 15

Chapter 3   –   Who Is This Really About? 21

Chapter 4   –   In What Business? 27

Chapter 5   –   Getting Our Heads Together 35

Chapter 6   –   Our Capability Lacks Credibility 41

Chapter 7   –   Revisiting Our Purpose 47

Chapter 8   –   A Hard Look 53

Chapter 9   –   The Relationships to Business 57

Chapter 10   –   Seeing Things My Way 65

Chapter 11   –   Moving Up and to the Right 71

Chapter 12   –   Out of Time? 79

Chapter 13   –   The Next Level! 87

Chapter 14   –   Looking Up 93

Chapter 15   –   A Candid Community Conversation 99

What Do I Do Next? 109

About the Author 110

Your Feedback Please 111

Introduction

Getting to the Next Level is a candid conversation about the real challenges and the opportunities of minority business development. Early readers of the book thought the conversation may even be too candid for some. Of course others thought the book was right on and shared the message how it should be shared. The fact is *Getting to the Next Level* is what we have learned from the minority entrepreneurs that have done it, the corporations that are truly committed to it and the communities that have invested in it. I agree it is candid and important insights are often tough to hear. The question is should those insights be shared anyway? We have decided that they should be. The goal is not to offend, accuse or excuse anyone. The goal is simply to share the insight we have gained from the work that we do.

Getting to the Next Level is based on our latest research on minority business growth, our recent work in communities around the country and our intense interactions with major corporations. The book shares what we say about each other that we are rarely willing to say to each other. It tackles the thorny issues head on including the role of special programs, the responsibility of major corporations, the mission of community groups like chambers of commerce and the responsibility of the minority business owner. It is a roadmap for changing what we do, how we plan and how we identify our success.

Most of all *Getting to the Next Level* defines what is next in minority business growth. What it will take. How it will work. What we must understand and how we must take action. The characters in this book are all fictional, but do not be surprised to find yourself and others that you know in these pages. The story is purposefully short and designed to be entertaining. The content is factual, well researched and based on the latest realities. The lessons are real. The activities are practical. The call to action is critical.

This book is not about special programs or spending goals or levels of commitment but yet in some ways it is. It is about business plans, growth strategies and competitive advantage yet in some ways it is not. The purpose of this book is to inspire us to focus on our common goal to be competitive. This book is about our collective next level of aspiration, expectation and thinking.

There is no doubt we have made progress in minority business development. Even more significant and lasting progress is possible and quite honestly imperative. This book articulates a conversation whose volume has been increasing over the last three years. The message is simple. Access is essential but not sufficient. There is another level.

Turn the page and discover what *Getting to the Next Level* really means.

What does this mean?
Are we about to lose the account?
Can we survive if we do?

CHAPTER 1

AM I LANDING
OR TAKING OFF?

Fenton settled into the comfortable chair in the Airline Club Room at the airport. He was tired and ready to get back home. After all, he had been gone for almost a week and he missed his wife and his children. The executive education seminar he had just attended was outstanding. He and the other business owners were exposed to a lot of new ideas and perspectives. Fenton had attended other education sessions in the past, but this one was different. The total focus was on getting to the next level. The pre-work and the class structure allowed each executive to apply the concepts specifically to their own business, their own industry and their own opportunities.

The sessions forced him to think and to reflect, and provided a magnifying glass on his business. Some of the outcomes made Fenton uncomfortable. He often felt his firm was not measuring up. He had been in business for 17 years and his business had grown. To the outside world he was successful. He had employees; he received awards; he served on boards;

he was a respected member of the community. But this session let him know that some things in his business were not right. It was like feeling something was wrong with your health and not hearing the details from the doctor. His business was sick; probably not terminal, but far from healthy.

He pulled the notes of the final session from the breast pocket of his jacket and began reading. *Signs You're At The Next Level,* he had written across the top. *1. Financial Success & Flexibility, 2. Ability to attract top talent, 3. Ability to attract capital, 4. Sought out by others because of market advantage...*

Signs of Being at The Next Level

1. Financial Success & Flexibility
2. Ability to attract top talent
3. Ability to attract capital
4. Sought out by others because of market advantage
5. Unique & clear value proposition
6. Evidence of ability to compete in free market
7. Wealth creation
8. Perpetuating business model
9. Winning competitive industry awards

Fenton felt his cell phone vibrating in his blazer pocket. It startled Fenton and jolted him away from his reading. He fumbled with the phone trying to figure out how to answer it. "Fenton Rice," he answered in a rushed voice.

"Still trying to figure that phone out, huh?" the voice on the other end questioned.

"I'm glad it's you." It was Michelle, Fenton's Chief Operating Officer. She was one of his most talented executives. They had been together since the beginning. She had seen it all and lived it right along with Fenton. She was loyal, more than capable and they were friends. "Yeah, you know I just got the thing last week. I'll figure it out. What's going on?" Fenton asked.

"I just got a call from Republic. They sounded upset."

"What do you mean upset? What's the problem? Have you gotten Jim involved?"

Republic was Fenton's largest and longest standing client. Jim was one of Fenton's most experienced executives, and he was Republic's account manager. They were a demanding client but reasonable and had really done a lot to help his firm grow. Losing them would not be good.

"They weren't specific. They just said they were concerned about our ability to serve their needs. They asked for a meeting with YOU next week."

"What does my calendar look like..." Fenton paused. "It doesn't really matter what my calendar looks like. We have to make room to meet with them."

"Already done," Michelle responded. Jim and I set the meeting for Tuesday morning. We thought we'd need a day to figure out what's going on and to prepare for the meeting."

"Good thinking. Thank you. Tell me, how upset did they sound?" he asked.

"Fenton, you know how they are. It's tough to tell. It just

doesn't feel good to me. I don't know what's going on but the situation sounds significant."

"Ok. I'll look into it. Anything else?"

"That's it," Michelle responded.

They hung up and Fenton's mind began to race. *What does this mean? Are we about to lose the account? Can we survive if we do? Maybe they just want to talk. No,* he thought. *It sounds like more than just a talk.*

"Excuse me. Is this seat taken?" a female voice asked.

Fenton looked up and saw a familiar face. "Hey Lourdes. No, of course not. Please, sit down."

Lourdes was an attractive woman with a friendly but business-like manner. She was the CEO of a staffing firm operating primarily in the southwest. She too had attended the executive education program. Lourdes lowered the briefcase from her shoulder and took the seat next to Fenton. They shook hands.

"What did you think of the class?" she asked.

"It gave me a lot to think about and many things to work on." Fenton replied. "What did you think?"

"I feel the same way. So many things to think about. I have to sift through it all and determine where to start." She sat back in the seat and looked out into space. "So much information can be overwhelming."

"Yes, it can be and already I'm back into the day-to-day grind of business," Fenton replied. "I just got a call from my office about an issue with one of our largest clients. And it'll get even crazier when we're actually back in the office."

"These training opportunities are great. I always leave enlightened, motivated and challenged," Lourdes confessed. "Then the daily race kicks in and there's just no time to pursue any real substantive changes to the business."

"I agree." Fenton said, his mind drifting again to his own issues and the questions about Republic. *I am not going to have time to do anything except get this problem fixed,* he thought.

Fenton reached forward to the bowl of snacks on the coffee table in front of them and put a few nuts onto a small plate. Three others, who had served on a panel during the last day of the executive education program, approached the two of them.

"Hello," Lourdes said. "Won't you guys join us?"

"Great panel discussion today," Fenton said as the newcomers sat down. "It was more informative and candid than we are used to hearing."

Lourdes nodded her head in agreement.

"Thanks," replied Ruth. She was a representative from a major manufacturing company. "We rarely get a chance to really tell it like it is to a group of minority business owners in a group setting like this one."

"It was our pleasure to be with you all," added Rob. He was the president of a Chamber of Commerce from a medium sized Midwestern community.

"There is a role for each of us to play. The better we play our role, the better results we'll all achieve," Marcus added. He was the director of the Minority Business Accelerator housed in the Chamber of Commerce in a large community.

"A role for each of us," Fenton repeated as a question he was still thinking through. "Marcus, what do you mean by that?"

"Well, I just think we sometimes forget that our individual roles are not the only roles needed to create the impact we all desire in minority business development. We can't just keep creating programs and put them on an island by themselves unconnected with the heart of commerce, and wonder why they don't work," Marcus replied.

"I agree," Rob added. "We all say it's about business but minority business development efforts often operate outside the mainstream of business activity. But the mainstream of business is where you get new customers, build entrepreneurial networks, develop actionable relationships, and birth new ideas," Rob said as he scanned the group, looking for their agreement.

"If it is about business, our behavior should demonstrate that we really expect it to be that way. Where we are with minority business is no one's fault but it is an opportunity for all of us. The group of us here is a microcosm of the environment at large. Our roles are clearly different but we are all actually after the same thing."

"What do you think that is?" Lourdes asked.

Fenton looked at his watch. He had time before his flight. He had a lot on his mind but this conversation was just getting good.

"Well," Rob said starting to explain "We all want…

CHAPTER
2

THERE'S A ROLE
FOR EVERYONE

"We all want competitive diverse businesses. We all want firms that create jobs and wealth. We want businesses that create value and serve their customers' needs. We all want firms that give back to the communities in which they do business."

The group nodded their agreement.

Rob continued. "Like Marcus said earlier, to have growing, sizable, successful and ultimately competitive minority owned firms everyone must play their part. There is a community role, a corporate and individual organization role and a minority business role," he said, drawing three circles and connecting them with a single line on the napkin in front of him.

Each of them has things they must do well. Rob continued. "The role of the community is to set the tempo and to create the environment. For example, our Chamber has to take the lead if we really are to be the center of commerce

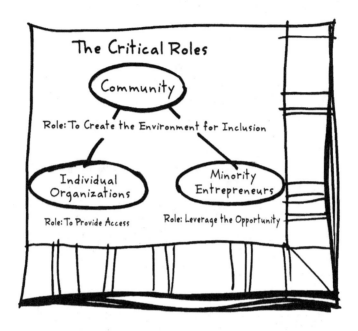

The Critical Roles

Community

Role: To Create the Environment for Inclusion

Individual Organizations

Minority Entrepreneurs

Role: To Provide Access

Role: Leverage the Opportunity

for the entire community. I hate when people refer to us as the "white" chamber. Of course it isn't true but what it means is that we aren't completely fulfilling our mission of being the central place where the entire business community comes together. Again, if it's really about business then chambers and other community business groups must play their role."

"Our Chamber won't touch minority business with a ten foot pole," Lourdes added.

"Why do you think that is?" Marcus asked.

"I haven't asked the question but I think it's partially because they fear the backlash from their non-minority members. Partially because they see minority business issues as a social problem and leave that work to traditional social service organizations. They don't see it as an economic opportunity, so why should they invest?"

Fenton chimed in, "I think they also fear a backlash from minority organizations, both business and social service. Chamber participation in minority issues is often seen as an intrusion on the turf of minority groups."

"When you say turf, what you really mean is intrusion on their budget dollars," Ruth said sarcastically.

"Yes, that too," Fenton conceded smiling at her candor.

"The individual major organizations in a community also have a role to play," Rob said pointing to the next circle on his drawing and continuing his explanation. "Businesses and other major organizations like universities and hospital systems are persuaded the most by their peers, especially when it comes to challenging and potentially controversial issues."

"Their role is also to find a way to include minority owned firms in the process," Rob said. "Their role is to know that our country is not at a point where it will happen naturally. The role of major organizations is to understand the long-term positive impact of a truly inclusive business environment."

"There is a lot of debate about which role is most important," Marcus offered.

"There shouldn't be any debate," said Ruth, the representative from the major manufacturing company. "The minority entrepreneur's role is to leverage their opportunity into their success. We have been dodging the truth too long. The biggest burden of success for minority owned firms must rest with the minority business owner."

Marcus cleared his throat to talk. "We've been dancing around this issue because we don't want to get accused of blaming minority firms for where they are. We can't afford to appear like we're not interested in improving the situation for minority owned businesses."

"Well my experience tells me that the successful minority owned firms feel they're at the center of their own success. No one has more responsibility than they do. And because of that thinking, those firms behave differently," Ruth said leaning back in her seat holding her hands up as she talked.

"And they get different results," Marcus added.

"You're right. It doesn't take away the important role of the rest of us, but without the minority businesses owning their own success, there isn't much you can do to help," Ruth concluded.

Fenton and Lourdes just listened. They were the objects of the conversation. Fenton had no idea what Lourdes was thinking but the conversation was a little uncomfortable. Every minority business owner he knew understood their role. They were committed to their own success. They pursued quality and opportunities to add value. Their problem was not their own commitment but the inconsistency of commitment from the other two roles. But the fact was that these people represented the organizations that had gotten great results in minority business development. They were just talking about what they learned in their experience. They all had track records that gave them significant credibility.

I asked and now I have to be ready to hear what they are telling us, Fenton thought.

"No matter our role, or our perspective or even our motivation, we all want successful minority owned firms," Ruth concluded.

"Do you really believe that?" Fenton asked. "Do you REALLY BELIEVE everyone wants minority firms to succeed?"

"Yes, I do. Where we often differ is to what effort we should go to make that happen. A person that looks like they don't get it may simply be a person who doesn't agree with the extent some people want to go. Very few people want to see any business fail."

"Minority business development does demand an investment of resources," said Marcus. "As in most investments, some people don't think the return is worth it. It doesn't make them racist or sexist or whatever. It's just how they see it. If we were honest, we'd admit that the promise of minority business growth is not new. If they perceive returns have historically been limited, then why should people believe it this time?"

"I hear that challenge all the time in my company. *Is all of this attention really worth our time and money?*" Ruth said.

19

"Then how do we convince those who don't believe?" Lourdes asked.

"By everyone playing their role one deal at a time," Rob replied. "A party grows based on the amount of fun the party creates."

Fenton looked at his watch. It was time for his flight to board. He shook hands with everyone, grabbed his bag and headed for his gate. *Interesting stuff,* Fenton thought as he walked through the airport terminal to his gate. *I have so much on my mind right now. And I've got to figure out what's going on with Republic. That's where I have to focus.*

CHAPTER
3

WHO IS THIS
REALLY ABOUT?

Fenton glanced at the clock on the wall. *11:25, man this has been a long meeting,* he thought.

They were all in a conference room with a large oblong table that could seat 15 people. The chairs were experienced and the carpet was a bit worn. There were scratches on two of the walls where the chairs had banged against them over time. The meeting included five people from Republic and three from Fenton's company. Fenton knew them all. Carol was one of the people from Republic. She was a tall fair skinned woman in her mid-forties and always well dressed. Fenton hadn't seen much of Carol in the last few years but they had a long history together. Carol had been his banker when he was starting his business and before she came over to run the minority business program at Republic. It was Carol who had introduced him to Republic and Carol who had helped facilitate his progress as a supplier. She had been his biggest supporter.

Fernando Pena, a respected vice president from the Florida region of Republic, was talking. Fenton had known Fernando for a few years. There was something about him that always bothered Fenton. He was always the most critical and the most difficult to satisfy. He seemed to be bothered by being *forced* to do business with minority owned firms. He always seemed to be looking for something he wanted that Fenton's firm could not deliver. He was a guy that most people would say just didn't get it.

Fernando was going through his concerns point-by-point; "We have discussed a number of topics but they come down to our concerns about billing accuracy, pricing, responsiveness, use of the latest technology and ability to provide service in international markets." He was polite but serious. It appeared he was agitated. Fenton did not agree with everything Fernando was saying. *So is it Fernando or Republic that has a problem with us,* Fenton wondered.

With every new thing Fernando mentioned Fenton got increasingly angry. *Some of the requirements he says he needs are really things he's using because he knows we don't have them. He's making his wants into needs as a way of shutting us out. That's nothing new,* Fenton thought fighting the urge to defend his firm. He knew appearing to be defensive never worked out well.

Carol just sat on the side and listened. Fenton could not tell what she was thinking. When Fernando finished Carol took over.

"We appreciated you all coming in today. We realize this is a lot to consume. Our business is changing and we need our suppliers to understand and respond to those changes."

"We understand," Fenton replied. Fenton was fuming as the group rose from their seats to leave the room. He was trying hard not to let it show.

"You have 60 days to give us your plan to address these issues," Fernando said as he left the room. "That's all the time we have."

"We got it. We'll be ready," Fenton replied now about ready to explode.

The others from Republic shook Fenton's hand as they left the room. "Let me know if there's anything I can do to help," Sandra, one of the high level project managers, said in a reassuring way.

Fenton and his colleagues left the conference room and began to walk down the hall toward the elevator.

"Fenton," a voice called.

It was Carol.

"Do you have a minute?" she asked.

"Sure Carol. You guys go on," he said to his colleagues. "We can talk when I get back to the office."

Fenton turned and followed Carol to her office.

"Have a seat," she said pointing to a chair across from her desk as she rounded it and sat in her chair.

"I wanted to make sure you understood what was going on."

"I think we're beginning to get it," Fenton said with a tenor of sarcasm. "We just had a three and a half hour meeting. The fact that you guys have concerns is crystal clear. I just get tired of the hoop jumpin'." Fenton's frustration was clearly beginning to show. "I've been a supplier here for years. You used me as a poster child to show your commitment to minority business. When you needed someone to be on a panel and speak in public forums to illustrate your willingness to do business with minority owned firms, I did it. I thought we had finally gotten there with you guys. This is why people wonder if you're *really* interested in doing business with minority owned firms."

"I guess you don't get it," Carol responded leaning up putting her elbows on her desk. "Our commitment to diversify our base of suppliers hasn't changed. If anything we are even more committed. But we *aren't* committed to compromising our success to do business with minorities."

Fenton was already upset and this conversation was clearly going in the wrong direction.

"Carol, you and I have been at this too long to go there. Now you are saying that doing business with minority owned firms means you have to sacrifice quality?"

"You know that's not what I'm saying. Fenton, you've lost perspective. I don't care if you get offended. Someone has to tell you the truth. It's not just you and your firm. Many of our suppliers have been programmed into thinking this is about them. Too many have taken our overtures to do business with diverse suppliers as our end game or our mission. We need competitive suppliers to help *us* be more competitive."

Fenton just listened. He was too upset to respond.

Carol continued. "Fenton, this is and always has been about us and about what we need. We're the customer. You're here to serve our needs. We're under increased pressure to compete, therefore you are under more pressure to help us be competitive."

"Are you saying we've not been a good supplier? Are you saying the only reason we're here is because we're a minority firm? What are you really trying to tell me?" Fenton asked.

"I'm trying to tell you we're about to find out. I'm trying to say that the focus on our supply chain has never been higher. We're consolidating the number of suppliers, increasing expectations for performance and evaluating our supplier options on a global basis. I'm trying to tell you that your ability to play your role to make us more globally competitive will determine your future with us."

Carol leaned back and sighed heavily. "Fenton, you stopped going to the next level. You stopped getting better. You stopped trying to find new ways to make us better. You just expected more and more business. Maybe it's my fault. If it is, consider this my attempt to make it right. I believe in you because I know the entrepreneur I met years ago. You were on the brink of disaster but you were also determined. I remember the entrepreneur who valued critical feedback and saw it as a way to improve. I know that guy and you better get reacquainted with him soon."

There was not much Fenton could say. He was bothered by the attacks. He was offended by the tone and frustrated by the reality. All those years of working and investing and sacrificing and he felt just like he did when he started.

The two shared a few more comments. Fenton thanked Carol for her comments, shook her hand and left. He wasn't sure he was thankful but he also didn't know what else to say. He made his way to his car, got in and sighed.

"What the heck is going on," he said aloud. "It seems like all of a sudden I'm getting the feeling we're doing everything wrong."

He started his car and drove back to the office to talk to his team about what to do about Republic.

CHAPTER 4

IN WHAT BUSINESS?

The sun was beginning to set in the early fall sky.
Fenton had just started his 40 minute drive home
after a long and challenging day. He thought about
his conversation with Lourdes about how the grind of the
day-to-day business rarely let them get to the point of actually implementing any of the concepts they'd learned. The new
ideas and fresh thoughts from last week's executive education
already seemed so far away. He and the management team
had been meeting most of the afternoon. They went through
the points one-by-one, evaluating their validity and discussing potential responses. Republic had outlined their specific
concerns but it felt like Fenton and his team was missing
something. *What's the real problem?* Fenton thought. *What
has changed all of a sudden? What do they really want from us?*
The management team had many ideas but they all seemed
to be treating the symptoms and missing the real problem.

Fenton looked at his watch. It was 6:45. He remembered
that his long-time advisor Hugh Belden often spent his

evenings in the park feeding the birds. It was time for one of those conversations. He took a left turn at the next street and was at the park in minutes. He took off his tie, rolled up his sleeves and began the short walk to Hugh's favorite bench.

Fenton did not know much about Hugh, just that he had been an extremely successful entrepreneur and that he had a way of making you think deeply. He could see him sitting as he approached. Hugh was a small and always neatly dressed Black man. Fenton could not help but notice how good Hugh looked. He had not aged a bit.

"It's a beautiful evening, Hugh," Fenton said sitting down on the bench.

"Well, hello, Fenton," Hugh replied with a big smile. "This is quite a surprise."

"Hugh, how are you?"

"I'm well, Fenton. I haven't talked to you in a while."

"I know. I've been so busy and time just seems to fly by. I'm sorry I haven't been in contact."

"Fenton, you know you never need to apologize to me," Hugh said, looking straight forward, slowly throwing food to the birds. "I understand what you're doing, and you know you always have my support. Stop apologizing and tell me what's going on."

"Hugh, I think we're about to be in it again. We had a very long and very difficult meeting with Republic, our oldest and largest client today. I knew they were upset when they demanded I personally be in the meeting. They're concerned about our ability to serve their needs going forward. They laid out a number of specific issues but there just seems to be more to it."

"Uh...huh," Hugh responded to indicate he was listening.

"I've had this feeling before and it's not good. I attended an executive education session with other minority business owners last week. It really was an opportunity to benchmark my thinking and our business approach. I'm not sure we measured up well. Then this latest blow-up at Republic makes me think we may have lost our way. We're getting some contracts but I'm not sure we're getting any better. I'm concerned. Honestly, I think we'd be completely lost without our minority business status and that was never how we wanted it to be."

The two men were silent. All you could hear were the sounds of the park.

"Hugh, are you still with me?"

Hugh smiled broadly still looking straight ahead. "Oh, I've heard every word, Fenton. Let me ask you. What business are you in?"

"The core of our business is marketing services. But Hugh, you know that almost as well as I do."

"Sounds like you've gotten into a totally different business than the one you say you're in. You say you're in the marketing services business but it sounds like you've slipped into the *minority* business."

Fenton was silent. Hugh's comments bothered him but he'd learned not to respond emotionally. It worked best when he waited, listened and actually attempted to understand the thoughts completely.

"When you're in the minority business, the minority business system becomes your industry. You learn it. You build relationships in it. The strategies for success in the minority business industry become your strategies for success. Minority business programs can be like a sedative that can slowly put your competitive edge to sleep. It doesn't happen in one day or one month. It doesn't happen to every minority business, but it does happen to many."

"In the Minority Business," Fenton said aloud. The thought of it made him think. *Am I really spending more time with issues related to minority business development than I am with my actual industry? Am I working the minority business system to provide us access or has it become what my firm is all about? The fact that I even have these questions is probably not a good sign.*

Fenton sat on the park bench thinking in silence and Hugh was content to let him. Everything was pointing to a need to make a change; a need to reevaluate the business. The experience of the executive education started it. The conversation with the group at the airport about everyone having a role highlighted the issue again. Then there was the rough meeting they had with Republic and especially Carol's comments. Hugh's words were just driving the point home.

Fenton slouched down further into the bench. The park was a wonderful place to think. The men sat for a few minutes and neither said anything until Hugh broke the silence.

"What is at the heart of the minority business system, Fenton? Why do programs really exist?"

"Well, they exist to help minorities get access to opportunities," Fenton replied, not sure of where Hugh was going.

"Ok. So let's go through the process. You get into a corporation as a supplier using a minority program or you get a loan because of it or you gain any other access. That's good," Hugh said continuing to explain. "You get more business or more funding because of how you managed whatever you got the first time. So you grow. That's good."

Fenton nodded his agreement.

"You start to carry the banner for what a minority business should be. You're a success story. But at every level you still carry the baggage that comes from the fact that you got help in the first place."

"Since we got help people think we must have needed help," Fenton said thinking it through aloud. "And if we needed help we must be less ready and if we're less ready...Wow!

We can't go to the next level because we can't avoid the potential negative association of being a part of a special program."

"Sure you can. Fenton, getting to the next level starts with a fundamental shift that must happen to your thinking, your aspirations and your strategy," Hugh said using his fingers to count the three areas.

Fenton just sat listening hard and taking it all in.

"You must move from using the programs just to gain access to leveraging the access to accelerate your business," Hugh said as he made his way to his feet.

Fenton did not respond. He wanted to ask more questions, but he got the clear message that Hugh had given him all that he was going to on that day.

"This is all good news, Fenton," Hugh said gathering his things. "The insight you got from the executive education; your concerns; your questions; the challenge you're getting from Republic. It's a shame but few of us change until we have to. Sounds like you're there. Give yourself a chance to succeed. Get back to the business you're in."

By the time he finished his sentence he had already started his slow walk away from the park bench. Before long he had disappeared down the meandering asphalt path.

Fenton sat alone for a while processing what he and Hugh had just discussed. He replayed the conversations of the last few days in his mind. His feelings were beginning to change from anger and frustration to a desire to take action and a sense of determination.

He reached for his PDA and began to type in notes.

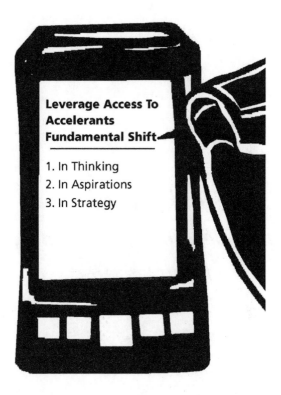

He reviewed his notes and began dialing the telephone number to his office. He was sure no one would be there but he wanted to leave a group voicemail message for the management team. They needed to meet the next day and begin to sort through their strategy.

Hugh was right. *It's time to give ourselves a chance to really succeed*, Fenton thought.

*We all know this stuff
but it has not often translated
to our actions.*

CHAPTER
5

GETTING OUR
HEADS TOGETHER

"This is bull," Tom, the company Chief Financial Officer said in frustration. "They're changing the rules in the middle of the game."

The other four members of the management team were present; Michelle, the Chief Operating Officer; Clyde, the Vice President of Marketing and Sales; Jim, the Vice President of Services and the executive responsible for the Republic account, and Fenton.

Michelle spoke next. "Well now, some of the concerns they have are legitimate issues and things we should have addressed a long time ago. I agree they are reaching on some others but Fernando seems to be speaking for Republic. The question is what are we going to do?"

"Fenton, I think you ought to go straight to Phil Price, the CEO. You have a relationship with him. He'll give you a meeting," Jim said.

"And tell him what, Jim?" Clyde asked. "That we don't like the way his people talked to us? Do you want Fenton to tell him that his people don't know what they're talking about? That they're racist? What would you have him say?"

"I don't know for sure but since we have the executive access I think we should use it," Jim said. "If we don't, we might just lose this account. Tom hasn't run the numbers yet, but I think we all know that it would not be good."

"What does Republic lose if we lose this account?" Fenton asked.

The four of them paused to ponder the question.

"What do you mean, what do they lose?" Clyde asked.

"Well, that might be the crux of the matter. Do they lose anything if they no longer do business with us? If not, then why should they care? Why should they keep us? Why should they compromise on anything they want just to do business with us?"

"Well, they'll lose some of the minority spending allocated toward their goal," Jim said.

"They may also get a hit to their reputation related to their commitment to minority business," Tom offered.

"That's what they're trying to tell us," Fenton said, ignoring Jim and Tom's comments, and acting as if he had just unlocked a secret puzzle. He was thinking about what he and Hugh had been talking about. "They're telling us that these programs can't make us competitive. The access is designed for us to leverage it to accelerate our progress to the next level. But the programs can't get us there."

"Fenton, I agree, and that's how we started out years ago," Michelle said. "But lately our focus has been more on using our minority status to get contracts."

"I'm not sure that's completely true," Clyde said. "We've discussed being world class and about being an industry leader. We talk about our unique value proposition."

"Yes, but what do we do about it? Do we measure our success that way? We all know this stuff but it has not often translated to our actions," Michelle said.

"Let's just look at it," Fenton suggested. "What have our last three or four big initiatives really been about? How about our joint venture with OVP? Why did they want to partner with us?"

No one responded. They all knew the answer.

"How about the alliance we created with Fase3," Fenton continued, seeming to have caught a rhythm. "What was their motivation? What was ours? I am not against joint ventures or strategic alliances or any other form of partnering with other firms. I'm just using those cases as examples. The same goes for other business we've pursued. You remember the big proposal we did for QStrike? What was our core value proposition to them? Cost reduction?

Quality improvement? Better delivery? No, we were showing them how they could increase their level of minority spending."

"Ok, I think we get it," Clyde conceded.

Fenton continued. "The programs can't make us competitive, guys. There may have been a time when they could," Fenton said, shaking his head. "But they surely can't anymore."

"Wait a minute, Fenton. We don't want to get this all out of perspective. These organizations all have goals and we always hear how they can't find enough qualified minority owned companies. Qualified minority firms like ours are in demand," Tom replied.

"But that demand isn't real. It's more like faux demand," Michelle said.

"Faux demand?" Clyde asked as they all laughed.

"Yeah, you know fake, imitation. It's not real. It's aspirational demand. They *want* to do more business with minorities but for the most part they don't *need* to."

"I think we're all saying the same thing," Fenton interrupted. "Whatever we call the demand, it is the demand we have access to. The minority business programs do have significant value but we can't let them become *our* only value. We have to find a way to leverage our access as an accelerant to increasing our *real* value to the customer."

"That's why we feel like the unwanted sibling in our relationships with our so called partnering firms. We don't really bring them enough core value. We're just there so that they can meet some minority requirement," Clyde added.

"Partnerships of any type should consider things like the exploitation of business synergies, gaining access to distribution channels and leveraging new technologies," Michelle offered. "Our proposals to our customers should be about the customer and what makes them better. What we can do to help them save money, make more money or serve their customers. Those should be our areas of focus. Our pursuit of adding new value is our leverage. That is when the minority business programs will be an accelerant to our success. Meeting the minority goals will be easier if we build value focused relationships."

"It's good news that there are goals to be met," Fenton said holding up his index finger to make his point. "Think about how powerful it would be if there were both a requirement to meet and a value driven reason to partner *beyond* the minority goal. We would have a bond that would really add value to both organizations and to our common customer. That has to be our goal."

"We have work to do to get this right," Clyde said.

"Where do we start?" Tom asked.

"We start with what Republic told us yesterday," Michelle suggested.

"That sounds like a good idea because we could have refuted most of the points Fernando made," Jim said. "There's no doubt that we've not been perfect. But no one is."

"That may be true but we were the ones in the hot seat yesterday. It was not a room full of suppliers. It was just us. They clearly have a problem with us and defending ourselves point-by-point does not seem like what they want to hear. I don't think they'd believe us anyway." Clyde said

"Tom, you're right," Fenton said. "We aren't as bad as Fernando presented and we could refute many of his points. But Clyde's point about their not believing us might be the best place to start. Why don't they believe us when we talk about our capabilities?"

CHAPTER
6

OUR CAPABILITY
LACKS CREDIBILITY

"Let's not fool ourselves," Michelle said. "Some of the issues are real. We've known about them for a while and haven't done anything to fix them. Our billing accuracy is a good example. We keep saying we'll get it fixed and then we get busy with the next contract. So part of the reason they don't believe us is because they have watched our behavior in the past."

"I think we also come with some baggage that's not our own. We are a part of a special program to help minority owned businesses gain access and for many people that means we're not capable," Clyde said.

"And everyone says they're capable. You have to say it if you expect to get the business. So how are they supposed to know who really is? Are we capable?" Tom asked.

The group paused. "Yes, we are," Michelle answered. "Like

any other firm, we have issues that need our attention but we are also quite capable of delivering to our customers."

"Fenton you said it before," Clyde added. "Our capability is lacking credibility. All businesses need credibility but minority businesses need it even more."

"I thought we'd grown past that already," Tom said. "We've been working with some of these companies for 10 years. We've proven ourselves to be capable. I didn't think our customers or our banker or the community still saw us as just a minority firm."

"You can think that if you want. Even you yourself just used minority firm in a way that is synonymous with less capable," Michelle explained.

"That's not how I meant it," Tom defended.

"Well it is how you said it and I think we all do it. Let's not be naïve enough to think others aren't," Michelle concluded.

Tom's comments were a sobering reminder to the group of how deeply ingrained the thinking about minority business really is. They all carry these thoughts in their minds and now they're beginning to see how it is affecting the business too.

"We can't go to the next level until our customers really see us as capable," Jim offered.

"We can't get our customers to see us as capable until we see ourselves as capable," Michelle said interrupting Jim.

"You're right, Michelle," Jim continued. "It really is more than just our customers. It's everyone. It starts with us and it must include our suppliers, our partners, our advisors; everyone must see us as *credibly capable*. Until they do, we'll always be marginalized and under scrutiny. It will be more about what we can't do well rather than what we can."

"So what will it take?" Fenton asked. "Why do they believe others are capable?"

"It is about what they see when they interact with us. We have to send consistent signals of credibility," Michelle replied. "Every interaction with the customer or banker or any stakeholder is an opportunity to send a signal. It will take time but sending consistent signals of credibility will begin to change the perception of our firm in a real and lasting way."

"I don't like it," Clyde said. "I don't like approaching our business assuming people think less of us from the start. It just feels like we're going backward in our thinking. People really have to begin to see us as a competitive business that just happens to be owned by a person of color."

"That's a great concept, Clyde, and I think we all agree they should see us that way," Fenton said. "But, if the reality is they don't, our job is to help them see at least our firm exactly as you described it; a business that happens to be owned by a person from a minority group. There are some things we don't like but also can't control."

Clyde shook his head. He did not like it. It felt wrong. It felt racist. It felt limiting but it also felt like the reality.

"So how do we send those signals of capability?" Fenton asked the group.

"It starts with the first interaction," Michelle said. "How we show up. From how we answer the phone, to the web site, to how our proposals look. It definitely includes the strength and accuracy of our financials. These are often the only things people see from us, and how they look starts their perception of us."

Fenton nodded at Michelle and Jim chimed in next.

"It's also about who you show up with and that starts with the strength of this management team."

"And our other advisors," Fenton added. "Our accountant, our lawyer and even our banker. Who they are and the quality of their work sends a signal that either contributes to the credibility of our capability or reinforces existing negative ideas about minority owned firms."

"Are you saying we have to dump our minority accountant and hire one of the major white accounting firms?" Tom asked.

"We never said they can't be minority," Fenton said. "We just said they had to be good. They have to enhance our credible capability. YOU made the connection that good must mean major and white."

"You're right," Tom said shaking his head. "That's exactly what I did. I never thought I really saw things that way but maybe I do," Tom explained.

Tom suddenly seemed uneasy and the others did not offer him much comfort.

Jim broke the moment of tension. "How we handle our business is also a signal of our credibility. If we appear to be out of gas, it confirms the predetermined belief that we lack capacity. If we miss deadlines, ship orders late, or show up unprepared, it confirms their thinking. When that happens what we say about our capability doesn't matter much."

"It just gives them a chance to say, *see I told you, they aren't ready to do business.*" Clyde added.

"But we have to be careful," Fenton said, sensing that the group was becoming too cynical. "It is true we can do a lot to contribute to the credibility of our own capability but we don't want to go so far that we start thinking people really don't want to do business with us. That's not healthy either. There's a fine line we can't afford to cross."

"Fenton, I thought we'd gotten past the need to prove ourselves," Jim said. "But in the proposals we've submitted and financing we've pursued, we've rarely gotten a chance to step beyond our current level."

"The good news is we are beginning to get a balanced view about why that is. Now we can do something about it." Fenton replied. "Starting tomorrow, we are going to do what we should have been doing all along. We are going to take a hard look at ourselves. The goals are to improve our capability and also give it more credibility."

They're right.
It's about them and every
other customer we have.

CHAPTER 7

REVISITING
OUR PURPOSE

Fenton and Michelle left the management team meeting at the same time and walked down the hall towards Fenton's office. As they approached his door Michelle asked. "Fenton, do you have a minute?"

"Sure," Fenton said as he stopped at his door.

"Fenton, the employees are waiting."

Michelle looked around and stepped into Fenton's office. Fenton followed.

"They're waiting to hear what you're going to do about Republic. They've heard the rumors. They see us running around and holding closed door meetings. They see we appear to be busy but no one knows what we're doing. They're waiting to hear from you."

"I know they are," Fenton said as he sat down behind his desk. Michelle sat in the chair across from him. "It's time we put our heads together on this. All of this feels so much bigger than just Republic. They're simply the wake-up call we needed."

"Fenton, that wake-up call is also our largest client. They helped us grow. It's with their help that we got other clients. We can't forget that."

"Oh, I haven't forgotten that, Michelle. We probably wouldn't be ready to make the changes we clearly need to make if it weren't for Republic pushing us," Fenton said, leaning back in his chair.

"I remember when we were just a six person firm and we were in the fight for our lives. You pulled the team together and reminded us that we had lost the art of entrepreneurship. We laid out a plan that day and we all recommitted ourselves to success. Fenton, it worked then and that approach will work again."

Fenton leaned back in his chair and looked up at the ceiling pondering Michelle's words and the content of the management meeting. He leaned his chair forward again.

"Let's call an all company meeting for 4:00 PM in the cafeteria," Fenton said.

Michelle smiled. She had seen that look from Fenton before. "Ok," she said. "By the way, do you have any idea what you'll say?"

"I know what we need to do," Fenton said with a wide smile. "And I have a whole 90 minutes to figure out how to say it."

Michelle left and Fenton turned his high back leather chair toward the window and again leaned it back. He reviewed the many things swirling through his mind. He was beginning to understand how his firm had gotten into this position and that understanding would serve as the foundation for finding their way out.

* * * * *

Fenton walked into the cafeteria with Michelle, Clyde, and Jim right behind him. Tom was already there. Every chair in the room was full and people were standing against the walls.

"Thank you all for coming on such short notice," Fenton said smiling. "I remember when we were so small we could've held this meeting in my office.

The group laughed softly.

He cleared his throat.

"You may have heard about our problems with Republic. To be honest, at first they really made me angry. But you know, they're right. We've been treating them, at best like they're privileged to be doing business with us and at worst, as a necessary nuisance."

Fenton paused and looked around. All eyes were on him and their faces reflected that they understood how serious a conversation this was.

"They're right. It's about them and every other customer we have. We've gotten flat and lost our focus on what they need, where they're going and what their challenges are. As long as they kept giving us contracts we were happy, and I led the way," he said tapping his chest with his finger to highlight his point.

"We're changing, and that change is beginning with me, and it's beginning today. I hope you'll all join me."

He approached a large, white marker board and grabbed a blue marker. Fenton looked around the room and then referred to a tri-folded piece of copy paper in his hand. He slowly put on his reading glasses and began to write and talk at the same time.

"The minority programs help give us access," he said drawing a graphic that appeared to be a sideways family tree he labeled *Access to Accelerants*. "We've been treating our access to these companies like access is the goal. It's not. It can't be if we are going to take our company to the next level. The real value of the access is the opportunity it provides to build on the business components that can really accelerate our success. Access provides us with things like cash flow, business contacts, systems and valuable experience," he said writing them on separate lines as he spoke. Leveraging our access to these accelerants has to become our focus. That's how we become more competitive and more able to add value to our customer."

"Each of these accelerants has their own potential value to us. For example, our business contacts," he said pointing to

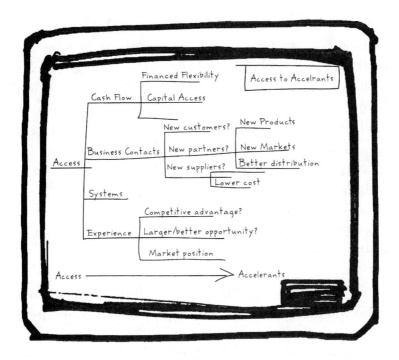

the graphic on the board, "they can lead us to new potential customers, new business partners and new suppliers."

We've been looking at this wrong. Our focus on managing the special access we get has made us miss the real value. We've got to open our eyes wider so that we see what the access really gives us. We can't build a competitive business based on getting access alone.

Fenton put the cap back on the marker and rubbed his hands together. He strolled back to the place he had begun his speech.

"That's what's next for us," he said pointing back to the board. "We need a plan to leverage our access. Over the next 30 days, the management team will lead us through the most comprehensive evaluation of our business we have ever performed. Nothing will be off limits. The outcome will certainly mean changes to how we do business. I don't know what that looks like yet, but I will guarantee you it will be about using our accelerants to get to the next level. It will be about being better positioned to serve our customers. We exist to help our customers be more successful. And it's *our* privilege that they do business with us."

He put the paper down. Pulled off his glasses and looked up.

"Join us. There's a role in this for each of us. I promise to keep you posted on the details as our plans become clearer. Are there any questions?"

Fenton responded to a few questions.

"Thank you all again for coming," he said. "Let's get back to serving our customers. Meeting adjourned."

Fenton tucked the paper into his breast pocket. He slowly walked over to talk to some of the employees to get their input and to address any individual concerns. Having this meeting was a good idea. He saw Michelle across the room. She gave him an affirmative smile.

Now we have to get to work, Fenton thought.

CHAPTER
8

A HARD LOOK

It was late in the evening. Fenton was still at the office. He and his team had been working on a comprehensive assessment of the business. The days had been long. Everyone was tired but they now had a real understanding of the issues, challenges and their opportunities for improvement.

He turned his chair around to face the laptop computer on the credenza behind his desk. He struck a few keys and settled in to type an email.

From: Fenton.Rice@FRGroup.com

TO: HBelden@Blam.com

Subject: Our look in the mirror

Attachment: Assessment Questionnaire

Hugh,

It has been a long three and a half weeks. We've been working 14 hour days to give our company the objective evaluation it deserves. I wanted to share the process and outcomes with you. We divided our review into five major categories. The first four you might expect; financial flexibility, operational effectiveness, strategic position, and marketing and sales. The fifth category was a careful review of how we were using the minority business development programs. Some of our assessment was quantitative and we compared ourselves to industry averages. Other parts of the evaluation were more subjective. In those cases we gave ourselves a grade based on what we knew to be the industry best. We then began to outline what it would take to improve in the areas that were sub par. Each area of improvement was prioritized based on how significant the impact would be on our ability to serve our customers, what we could improve relatively quickly and what we had the most control over improving.

For example, one of the glaring concerns with our financial flexibility is our accounts receivable. It is generally much higher than the industry average because we often send the customer bills that are incorrect. The incorrect bill slows them in paying us. The outcome is we have to take on more debt to cover expenses until we get paid. The expense of the extra debt increases our overall cost of doing business which makes us less competitive. You get the picture. We can fix the billing problem and we will. We found concerns like that throughout the business. Some simply take our focused attention to fix. Others will take significant investments of money and a longer time. At least now we know.

I am not sure I have ever been as clear about the state of our business as I am right now. We looked at everything with a customer orientation. We wanted to be candid with ourselves about how our customers really see us. We especially wanted to understand how we have REALLY been getting our new business and to what extent we relied on the minority business programs to make us competitive. By the way, through this process we also determined that Republic is such a large part of our business that we likely cannot make it if we lose that account. We clearly can NOT lose that account. Diversifying our customer base more will take time but again, at least now we know that has to be a priority.

It is exciting and challenging at the same time. We have work to do but at least we understand the work better. Thank you as always for taking the time to provide your usual push and direction. It always helps me think more deeply and to be more candid with myself. Talk to you soon.

Fenton

P.S. I attached the questionnaire we used to perform our assessment. I thought you might find it useful in helping someone else.

Fenton read his email over again. He made a few changes, pressed send and turned off his computer. He collected his things and headed toward his car to go home.

It was dark outside now as Fenton made his way up the familiar highway. He was thinking about the steps they had gone through and how prepared he felt they were to respond to the concerns Republic had identified.

His cell phone rang. Fenton was sure it was his wife calling. He pushed the button on his headset and answered. "Hey, honey. I'm on my way."

"Well, hey, Honey to you too," the male voice on the other end responded. It was Hugh.

"Sorry, Hugh, I thought you were Yvette. What's going on?" Fenton asked. It was unusual for Hugh to call him.

"Fenton, I got your email and want to get together with you soon to talk about a few things."

"Is something wrong?" Fenton asked, a bit puzzled by the urgency.

"There's nothing wrong. It just isn't complete," Hugh responded. "How about tomorrow at 7:00 A.M. in our usual place? It won't take long."

"Ok Hugh, I'll be there at 7:00."

"I'll see you then," Hugh said as both men hung up.

CHAPTER
9

THE RELATIONSHIPS
TO BUSINESS

It was a cool morning. The sun was just coming up and dew was on the ground. Fenton loved the mornings; especially fall mornings. The smell of the wet grass reminded him of his youth; of playing high school sports. He walked briskly through the park on his way to their usual bench. Hugh was already there.

"Good morning, Hugh," Fenton said.

"Good morning, Fenton," Hugh replied.

Hugh was wearing his usual overcoat and gentleman's hat but he did not have his birdseed.

Fenton sat down. "Hugh, what was so urgent?"

"Fenton, the work you guys have done on evaluating the business is good work. I looked at the assessment you used. It's well done. It's thorough, challenging and candid. You guys have a great start. But let me ask you this, how did your business get in this position?"

"We obviously took our focus away from getting to the next level. We just wanted to get the next contract," Fenton replied trying to answer the question completely but not knowing the answer Hugh was seeking.

"Did your loss of focus just start recently?" Hugh asked.

"No. It's obvious Republic's issues with us go back some time."

"Why are you just now hearing about them? Why did it get so bad that they had to give you an ultimatum and a deadline?" Hugh pressed.

"I don't know. No one told us before now," Fenton admitted.

"That's a problem, Fenton. The fact that no one told you until this point is as much a problem as their specific issues with your performance. You can *fix* the issues but it'll be just a matter of time before you're back in this position again."

"Hugh, we can't make them tell us something. This is a big company and we deal with a lot of different people," Fenton explained.

"Fenton, how did you get into the Republic account in the first place?"

"Carol, my long-time banker, left banking and went to Republic. When she moved to Republic she helped us get in."

"She introduced you to the right people? Told you about their priorities? She gave you feedback on what they thought of you? She gave you council on how you might be successful?" Hugh asked.

Fenton nodded his head. "Yes, she did all of that."

"Why did she do that Fenton? Did you make her?"

"Of course not," Fenton smiled now, beginning to see Hugh's point. "Part of it was her job and I'm sure most of it was our relationship," he admitted.

Hugh was right. They had not built the kind of relationships inside of Republic that provided an avenue for that kind of candid and often informal feedback. Fenton had not even spent much time with Carol in the last few years, let alone trying to build similar relationships with others.

"What about your relationship with Carol made her want to help?" Hugh asked.

Fenton paused and thought for a moment. "Hugh, Carol and I have been through it. We've worked on projects together. I've had to rely on her and her on me. We've had tough conversations with each other and realized we were both open because we both wanted to get better. She probably wanted to help because she knew what she would get from me. There was typically something in it for both of us, but that wasn't the real reason why. We have a good old fashioned business relationship."

"So part of it is how long you've known her and part of it is what the two of you have experienced together. These come together to form what she knows about you. She helped because she could and because what she knew about you made it easier. That's a business relationship."

Fenton looked straight ahead, thinking about the relationship with Carol and how it came to be that way. It was about trust and confidence that had been developed and nurtured over time.

"If you think about the success you've had over the years," Hugh said. "You'll find those kinds of relationships in your success. They were critical when I was running my companies and they're critical now. There is probably nothing more important in business than relationships."

Fenton was listening and thinking. He and his team had not talked about relationships but Hugh was right. All of their success was because someone was in a position to help and had the inclination to do so.

"Relationships," Fenton said aloud. "Maybe that would help us deal with people like Fernando Pena. He just doesn't get it. He's against the whole idea of minority business development."

"Is he really? How do you know that?" Hugh asked.

"From the way he behaves. We think most of the issues Republic has with us are really coming from Fernando," Fenton explained.

"Really?"

"Trust me. This guy is something else. We've gotten nowhere with him."

"Fenton, I'm not sure I understand what you're saying. What does this Mr. Pena say to you? What does he do? Start with your last conversation with him. How did it go?"

Fenton smiled the smile of a man that had been baited and hooked by one of the best. "I'm not sure I've ever had a direct conversation with him," Fenton admitted sheepishly. "If I have, it has not been anytime recently."

Hugh did not respond.

"I guess I really don't know what he thinks because it's been easier to *think* I already know. I have to get a meeting with Fernando, don't I?" Fenton asked.

"It might not be a bad idea," Hugh responded as he pressed his hat firmly on his head and stood up. "I haven't met many people who truly don't get it, Fenton. What does he know about you? What do you know about him? Doesn't sound like either of you know much? Relationships matter most," Hugh said as he walked away, leaving Fenton on the park bench. Fenton could see the sun through the trees as it made its way up for the day.

Relationships matter most, he thought as he reached into his coat pocket for his PDA. He began typing. Relationships: Time + experience + intensity = trust. *I think that's it,* he thought. He scrolled through the list of contacts in his telephone until he got to Fernando's number. He pressed the send key and the telephone began to ring.

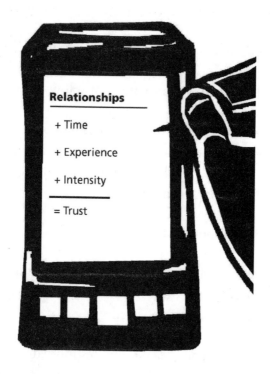

"Fernando Pena," the strong, business like and almost abrupt voice answered.

It was so early in the morning, Fenton was surprised that Fernando was in his office to answer the call.

"Fernando, this is Fenton Rice," Fenton replied.

"Yes," Fernando answered with a hint of Hispanic accent and as coldly as his initial voice.

"Fernando, I'd like to come to your location in Florida to meet with you about what we're planning to present as our response to the concerns Republic has with our performance."

"I don't think you and I need to meet, Fenton. We gave you our concerns in our meeting. When you're ready to formally respond we can all get together then."

"Fernando, you're right. But I think you, more than anyone, have a grasp of what it's going to take for us to be successful. We've done a lot of work internally and I'd like to get your input on our direction. I'm willing to come to you and I promise to only take 30 minutes of your time."

"You're going to fly two hours to spend 30 minutes with me?"

"Yes, I'll arrange other meetings during my trip but your input is that important to us."

"Ok," Fernando agreed. "How about Thursday in the early afternoon? It will give you a chance to fly in and out on the same day."

"Does 1:00 Thursday work for you?" Fenton asked.

"That's fine," Fernando said and the two men hung up.

Fenton emailed his assistant about the meeting from his PDA as he walked back to his car.

Fernando is a gruff guy, Fenton thought. *But it is better to know him and have him know us better than to not know him at all.* The meeting was set and Fenton knew it was an important one.

CHAPTER
10

SEEING
THINGS MY WAY

enton waited in the lobby for Fernando to come to get him. It was 1:15 and Fenton was growing annoyed that Fernando was late. As Fenton stood to ask the receptionist if there was a problem he could see Fernando walking briskly down the hall. He was a short, stocky man whose attire showed his focus on the bare essentials of life.

"Sorry I'm late," Fernando said. "We have a situation at one of our South American locations and the call went longer than I thought it would. I apologize."

Although the timing bothered Fenton he could not let Fernando know. "I understand," said Fenton. "I really appreciate your making time to see me."

"Come this way. I've reserved a small conference room."

The two men entered the room and sat down. "What do you have?" Fernando asked.

This guy has no personality, Fenton thought. *Everyone exchanges some pleasantries don't they?*

"I wanted to meet with you personally to get your feedback on our progress. We've been working on the specific actions needed to make ourselves more competitive suppliers to you here in the Florida region and to the rest of Republic."

Fernando just listened and nodded his head.

"Let me show you what we've done," Fenton said as he opened his table top presentation and turned it so they both could see. For the next 20 minutes Fenton presented a summary version of the strategy the management team had developed based on the issues Republic outlined and the internal assessment the team had performed. At first Fernando just listened and then he began to challenge almost every one of Fenton's ideas.

"Fernando, if you're looking for things we can't do, you'll always find them."

"I'm not trading on what we need, Fenton."

"What Republic *needs* or what *you* want, Fernando?" Fenton said his frustration clearly showing.

Fernando appeared surprised by Fenton's tone.

"Look," Fernando said, "it's no secret I'm not a fan of minority business development programs. I think they make our work more difficult. There's no doubt I have serious issues with your firm as a supplier to us. But people think it's about race with me. It's not."

"Then what *is* the problem?"

"Your firm is too small. And because you're so small you have limited resources. The limited resources are what make it a challenge to do business with you."

"That's what the minority programs are designed to help with," Fenton replied.

"Well, if that's true, that's a problem too. It's not supposed to be a perpetual game of minority firms getting special treatment and not get bigger or better and more capable. I thought the programs were designed to help minority firms get to the next level."

Fenton was upset with Fernando but intrigued by his well structured opinion.

"So what do you think we should do?" Fenton asked.

"You're small and I assume you want to be more competitive. Your plan, your business model and your overall approach should work with the reality of your limited resources. You can't sustain competitiveness doing business like you're doing it."

"I'm not sure I understand what you're saying. Give me some examples," Fenton requested.

"You're in at least four lines of business. You're honestly mediocre at best at any one of them. Mediocre won't get it and I suspect you're mediocre because your limited resources are spread too thin," Fernando explained.

"You're talking about the warehouse project we took on?" Fenton asked.

"And the light assembly site in Iowa." Fernando added. "We did it so that we could count the money we spend with you against our minority business spending goals. Why did you do it, Fenton?"

"We did it because it was an opportunity to drive some revenue and profit," Fenton replied. "It was an opportunity."

"Yeah, but did it make you better? Did it make you more competitive? If that's your approach to business, don't be surprised if you keep having problems meeting our needs," Fernando said.

Fenton just looked at him. He was annoyed. It felt like Fernando was talking down to him. *What does he know about running a business?* Fenton thought. *He's never taken the risk to run his own firm. It's easy to know all the answers when you have a cushy position and a steady paycheck.*

"Fenton, you can fix what's wrong with your billing, your responsiveness and even your pricing," Fernando said in a conciliatory tone. "But you'll at best just continue to exist. And the only reason you'll exist is because of the minority program. I'm sorry, Fenton. That's why I have problems with these types of programs."

"I appreciate your opinion," Fenton said wanting to move on. "What did you think of the presentation?"

"What you've done responds to our concerns and I won't stand in your way in the review meeting. Is that what you're asking?"

"Yes, that's part of what I'm asking. But your deeper concerns concern me too. Do you have suggestions for how we use the minority business programs to really go to the next level?"

"Fenton, Republic does work with a lot of smaller firms. As a matter of fact it is becoming more and more our strategy to find small, entrepreneurial and innovative firms that can do things better, faster and often cheaper than we can," Fernando explained. "I always wondered what the difference was between a small minority firm in need of help and a small innovative firm we want to invest in. Answer that question and I think getting to the next level will become less challenging."

"That's an interesting question. I'll give it some thought," Fenton replied.

The two men talked about potential dates for the review meeting with the whole group and a few other logistical issues as Fenton packed his things. They shook hands and Fenton walked down the hall and through the lobby. There was a driver waiting outside to take him back to the airport.

Fenton took his bag off of his shoulder and leaned back into the rear seat. He was not sure what to make of the meeting. At least he got Fernando's support. He was also struck by how candid Fernando had been. Why? What was in it for him? And that final question. *What is the real difference between a struggling minority firm and a small entrepreneurial firm?* Fenton thought.

Fenton remembered hearing that question before. It was in the executive education program. One of the presentations talked about that difference. *There is an article on the CD they gave us,* he thought. *I'll have to look that up. Even though I didn't like what Fernando said, I think he has something there.*

CHAPTER
11

MOVING UP AND
TO THE RIGHT

The flight from Florida seemed to take just minutes. Fenton's mind was racing as he left the plane. He walked down the terminal corridor and out the airport doors to the parking deck. He was curious and wanted to take a look at that article. It was 6:00 P.M. He started his car and headed straight for his office.

Fenton was seated at his computer scrolling through the table of contents of the CD from the class. There were topics on entrepreneurship, business model development, mergers and acquisitions and managing a fast growth company. "There it is," he said aloud. "Why Can't Minority Firms Be the Best?"

He double clicked on the title and began to read.

> Almost all minority businesses are small businesses but rarely are they seen as the revered small entrepreneurial firm. They are rarely the firm that is seen

as so nimble and so quick that they out fox larger companies and provide most of the real innovation to the market place. Minority firms rarely attract attention because they have found a better way of doing something or because they have effectively exploited a niche. They do not attract investment in their ideas, or processes or their new technology.

Although firm size, scale, resources, and funding are often similar, minority firms are more likely to be associated with being poor laggards in need of help to sustain themselves. The question is: why is this true? The answer is complex and some of the issues are out of the direct control of the minority firm. Things like how minority firms are perceived in general and the firm's access to entrepreneurial networks. There is no doubt these are factors. But potentially the most significant factor is within the control of the entrepreneur. It is the aspiration of the minority firm. Few entrepreneurs of color aspire and therefore plan to be industry leaders or innovators.

I'm not sure I completely agree but I understand his point, Fenton thought. He read on.

This is not an indictment of minority firms but it is a reality that limits profitable growth and market impact. For the purposes of this article we define entrepreneurial and innovative firms as those that are both difficult for customers to replace and have a high ability to make their customers better. The Market Position Four Quadrant Model found in Exhibit

A provides a simplified, two dimension description of market position. Four quadrants emerge when the market is viewed based on the relative ease for your customer to find suitable replacement options (y axis) and the extent your product makes your customer better (x axis). Although this is a simplified view it does present a way of thinking about the business you are in and how it affects your ability to be seen as an innovative and entrepreneurial firm.

Minority firms are heavily positioned in quadrant three, followed by quadrant four. This means that minority firms are primarily in businesses that are easy for the customer to find suitable replacements. The reality of having plenty of replacement options often drives down profitability, shortens the length of contracts and the means of competing is often found in the form of size and scale. The idea is simple. The more real options the customer has, the lower they expect the price to be. Minority firms typically do not have size or scale and do not lead in price. Therefore, sustainable success is difficult in quadrants three or four without special minority business programs.

Fenton stopped reading and looked at the four quadrants. He mentally plotted their various business areas on to the chart. "We are in quadrants three and four," he said to himself. That's what Fernando was saying to me, he thought. In those quadrants scale is important to him. He skipped the part describing quadrants three and four and went straight to the section of the article with the heading of Making Every Quadrant Work.

73

The Market Position Four Quadrant Model

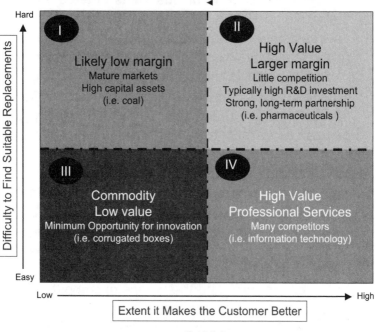

Exhibit A

The obvious answer appears to be to get in a business that is in quadrant two. That is where all of the differentiation is. That quadrant has the least amount of competition. That is the quadrant where your customer will seek you out. But this quadrant is not for everyone. Plus there are successful businesses in all of the quadrants. There is an opportunity to be entrepreneurial and innovative in all of the four quadrants. The question is how? There are four steps that are simple to understand but often difficult to implement.

1. Understand the quadrant you are in. It is critical you honestly understand your current position.

You cannot plan to improve your position without being realistic about your current situation.

2. Understand the economic rules of the quadrant. For example, quadrant three is primarily driven by scale, size and price. Knowing this becomes the basis of your strategy.

3. Commit to being entrepreneurial and innovative. This commitment is more than just saying it is so. There are real operational changes that must take place that makes your firm always looking for ways to get better, faster, and cheaper within the economic rules of your quadrant.

The Market Position Four Quadrant Model

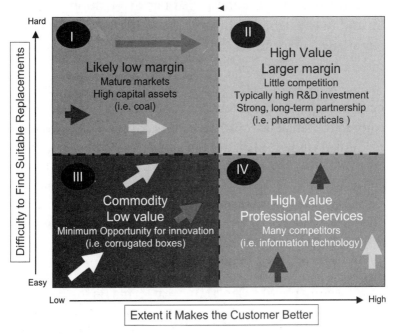

Exhibit B

4. Stay focused on moving up and to the right. As the arrows indicate in Exhibit B. It does not matter where you start. The real goal of being more innovative and more entrepreneurial is that it makes your firm more difficult to replace and more able to directly make your customer better.

Everyone cannot be in quadrant two. Nor should they want to be. Quadrant two has its own challenges. It also has tremendous barriers to entry and success. The goal should be to move your firm closer to the positive customer behaviors associated with quadrant two. Remember, you don't have to be more innovative or entrepreneurial than every other firm, just the firms competing in your quadrant.

Fenton stopped again and paged back to Exhibit B. Move up and to the right, he thought. That's a good challenge for our management to face. We have to find a way to work these concepts into our plan.

Fenton saved the article to his hard drive and printed a copy to the small laser printer on the corner of his credenza. He pulled up his email and began to type.

....

From: Fenton.Rice@FRGroup.com

TO: ManagementTeam@FRGroup.com

Subject: Why Can't We Be The Best?

Attachment: Why Can't Minority Firms Be the Best?

....

Team,

I realize we have been working long hours and have put a lot of ourselves into this process. We are almost there. We want to be sure we not only respond to Republic but actually use this process as an opportunity to become a better company.

The meeting with Fernando went as well as could be expected. He is a tough guy to read. He did challenge me on a few ideas that are not a part of our current plan. Basically he asked "why can't we be the best?" That is a good question and I think it warrants our attention. The attached article is a bit technical at times but I think it provides us with a structure to think about this question. Please review it in preparation for our management meeting tomorrow.

The review meeting with Republic is in just a few weeks. We have to be ready.

Fenton

Fenton turned off his computer and headed for home.

We're not giving up any part of this account or any other customer without a fight.

CHAPTER
12

OUT OF TIME?

Before Fenton knew it he was on his street, pulling into his driveway and then into the garage. As he parked the car his cell telephone rang.

"Fenton Rice," he answered.

"Fenton, it's Carol. I have bad news. I just got a call from Fernando Pena from our Florida region. He is pulling your contract with them in that region. Fenton, I don't have to tell you, Fernando is very well respected and others inside of Republic will likely follow his lead. It's a problem."

"I just met with Fernando earlier today and he said he wouldn't stand in our way. Plus I thought you guys gave us 60 days to respond," Fenton said.

"I thought so too. Something else must have happened. I don't think he's selected another supplier yet but he has made the decision that your firm is out. At least in Florida," Carol explained.

"Ok," Fenton said slowly thinking through his next steps. He felt calm for some reason that he could not explain. His thoughts were clear and unemotional. "Carol, I need your help. I understand that Fernando has made his decision. I need a chance to win the business back. We think we have the plan. Can you get us a meeting with the right people?" Fenton asked.

There was silence on the phone. "Carol," Fenton called.

"I'm here, Fenton. Of course, I'll do all I can to get you that meeting. I was just thinking about who I should call first. Try to get some sleep. I'll start making calls in the morning. Give me a few days. In the meantime you probably ought to find out what happened in Florida to send Fernando over the edge."

The two hung up, and Fenton was on his phone again calling each member of his management team. Their management meeting tomorrow had just taken on a new sense of urgency.

His last call was to Michelle. "Fenton, what are we going to do?" she asked.

"First thing tomorrow I'm going to call Fernando and find out what happened. Then *we're* going to reintroduce ourselves to him and the others at Republic and hope they'll take us back. We're not giving up any part of this account or any other customer without a fight. I'll see you in the morning. We're about to find out how much we've learned."

* * * * *

Carol pulled the meeting together in just a few days. Managers and executives from various locations of Republic were expected to be there. They were meeting in a large conference room at the Republic headquarters location. Fenton and his management team had entered the room early and set up the computer and projector in preparation for the presentation. They were ready. They had spent the last two and half days refining their plan. The general theme was based on being more valuable to the customer. There were short-term initiatives to address immediate issues and strategic plans to make the business more entrepreneurial and innovative. They made it clear that they had heard Fernando's question about being the best.

Some of their strategies were significant departures from their current business. For example, they planned to sell off non-core businesses like the light assembly plant in Iowa and the warehouse operation.

They had also made preliminary progress in identifying opportunities to enter into mutually beneficial partnerships that leveraged their strengths and not just their minority status. They identified existing partnerships that were not good for their business and a timeframe for ending those relationships.

The presentation was concise but comprehensive. It was responsive to the particular concerns Republic had presented but it went much further. Their concepts were bold but realistic. The ideas were thoughtful but full of the passion needed to actually make them happen.

For about an hour the team presented their plan. They fielded questions and responded with the poise that instills confidence. Yet they were candid about the realities and limitations of the firm. They admitted short comings when appropriate and fought not to be defensive. The Republic group challenged them hard on their ideas and asked the kind of questions rooted in skepticism. Fenton sat in the back and allowed the team to lead. He could see them winning the group over one-by-one. He was proud of his team, no matter the outcome of this meeting. They were going to be a better firm because of the work they had done.

The meat of the presentation was over and it was Fenton's turn. "Ladies and gentlemen, our companies have been doing business together for more than a decade. Much of our success with other customers has come because of our relationship with you. We lost sight of our role and took our eye off of you, the customer. We lost our edge and our ability to meet your changing needs. We get it now. This is and always has been about serving you, our customer. You've heard our plan. I know some of you have already made up your mind about us. Our recent warehouse mistake in Florida surely didn't help our cause. This presentation is our plan of what's to come. We know it falls short of real evidence of change but this is truly the best we can do. Today we're here to ask you for your business and to demonstrate our commitment to competing for your business everyday. We await your decision and we thank you for the opportunity."

Fenton could see Carol smiling in the back of the room. Fenton knew they had done all they could. The group exchanged hand shakes and collected their things to leave.

Fernando was one of the last people in the room. He was clearly waiting for his opportunity to talk with Fenton. Fernando approached. "Fenton, nice presentation. I have to tell you that it is too late for you guys in the Florida region. We're going with another firm there. We'll get back to you about your status with the other locations of Republic. I have to admit, I was impressed with how you listened and how you responded. I'll give you a call once we all have a chance to discuss your presentation," Fernando said with a subtle smile.

Fenton smiled back. "Thank you for coming and for your input. I'm glad you saw evidence that we listened. Your candor mattered," Fenton said.

They shook hands and Fernando left the room.

Carol walked up to Fenton as Fernando left. "Fenton, do you have a few minutes?" Carol asked.

Fenton motioned to the others in his group to go ahead without him. Carol and Fenton stayed in the conference room and sat down. "I have a few things to share with you," she said.

"Before you say anything I want to thank you, Carol, for getting this meeting set up for us," Fenton offered.

"No problem. You clearly played your role, Fenton. It made it easier for me to play mine. You and your team did a great job. By the way, that was a smart move going down to meet with Fernando ahead of time," Carol said.

"I agree. But his mind is made up about us right now. At least he knows that we want his input. I'll keep in touch with him as we have more evidence that we are delivering on the promises we made today," Fenton said.

"Fernando is used to hearing a good story and with no real action to back it up. He's jaded," Carol said shrugging her shoulders. "I think your willingness to listen to him and to incorporate his thoughts into your plan may be the foundation to building a strong ally. Fernando is a good guy."

"I'm starting to see that now, but it's hard to see when he's picking you apart," Fenton replied with a slight grin.

Carol smiled back. "Listen, I wanted to talk to you because I know I was tough on you when we talked after the first meeting. I also want you to know we realize we have a lot of work to do ourselves."

"I understand, Carol," Fenton replied. "I can't say it didn't bother me but I can say it was what I needed to hear at the time. You were right. This IS about the customer and we must continue to evolve as a competitive supplier."

"Our company's role with minority owned firms is also continuing to evolve. We have the basic systems in place but we have to do more. We're working on it," she said, shaking her head to indicate the amount of work still to be done. "It has to become a part of how we do business."

"Carol, thank you again for giving us this opportunity," Fenton said as he stood up. "No matter what they decide, you've done what you can and we have too."

"I was proud of you today. I really enjoyed watching you compete."

The two hugged warmly. Fenton felt reconnected with his friend.

"This worked out the way it was supposed to," Fenton said. "I was told that people don't change until they have to. We had to and we have."

"Oh, Fenton, I almost forgot," Carol said holding up her index finger. "The Chamber of Commerce is hosting a town hall meeting on the topic of minority business development next Thursday. They have an expert coming to town and Republic is the corporate sponsor. We'd love for you to attend."

"That sounds interesting," Fenton said thinking about the topic. "It also sounds like a healthy discussion for our business community to have. Sure. I'll check my schedule and try to make it. See ya later. Thanks again."

Fenton smiled and walked down the hall to the main lobby. The rest of the team was waiting. They were in a good mood. They deserved it. They'd worked hard to be ready.

"Can I buy you all lunch?" Fenton asked them as he walked up.

*We are a different company
than when this all started.*

CHAPTER

13

THE NEXT LEVEL!

It was early afternoon on Thursday and Fenton was on the telephone in his office. "I understand," he said into the receiver. "Yes, you told us we'd be replaced in Florida. Sure we can switch the order of those two priorities. Yes, we would appreciate some help from your packaging engineers on exactly how you want that setup. No, Jim will no longer be handling the Republic account. He is leaving the company. I'll get Kim Jones, our new VP of Services, involved with working through the details of the changes."

"Fenton, one more thing," the voice on the telephone said. "Again, I like your plan and I'm interested in seeing the results. Keep me posted on your progress. When the time is right, we'll see what we can do to get you back into the Florida region and some of our overseas markets."

"Thanks for your interest, Fernando. We will keep you posted. Thanks for the call," Fenton said hanging up.

Fenton pressed his lips together with a determined look and then a subtle smile. "There is a price to pay for falling asleep at the wheel," he said aloud, shaking his head.

He quickly turned to his computer and began to type an email to the entire company.

From: Fenton.Rice@FRGroup.com

TO: AllAssociates@FRGroup.com

Subject: Republic accepted our plan

Team,

I wanted you all to know as soon as I found out. Republic has accepted our plan to continue to be a supplier to their company. We were unsuccessful in convincing them to keep us in the Florida region. This loss of business will mean tough choices and changes for us. Our focus now must be on getting ourselves to the next level. We have done the planning part. Now we have to do the hard work of implementation.

We were challenged by our customer and we responded. Thank you all for your efforts.

Fenton

Fenton continued to check and return emails. About half way down the list was an email from Lourdes. Fenton double clicked on the note and quickly read it. He selected the reply button and began to type.

....

From: Fenton.Rice@FRGroup.com

TO: LBurton@LDSServices.com

Subject: How are things going?

Attachment: Access to Accelerant Tree
....

Lourdes,

Thanks for checking in, and especially for your concern about Republic. We presented our plan to them a few days ago and we just got word this afternoon that although we retained the account, we lost the Florida region. We simply did not deliver too many times. Losing that business is going to hurt. The good news is the results of the process we have gone through goes far beyond Republic. We are a different company than when this all started. We have made some tough decisions like deciding to sell off some of our non-core businesses and to exit some of our lackluster joint ventures. We plan to redeploy the resources currently tied up in those initiatives to strengthen our position in our core marketing operations. For example, we are aggressively pursuing partners with an existing infrastructure in strategic global locations. I also made some personally difficult decisions to make changes to our management team. Jim, our VP of Services, and Tom, our Chief Financial Officer, are both leaving.

They are friends of mine and good people. They were full of potential but have not been able to effectively play their role on the team.

We started with a comprehensive assessment of the fundamentals of the business. We looked at everything and what we found was not all good. I guess I would call it harsh but accurate. :) I have attached the assessment process and questions. You might find them helpful. We understand our business better from top to bottom and we are working everyday on the things that matter most to increasing our ability to compete.

I am proud of how we fought for the business. But most of all I am hopeful because of everything we learned about ourselves, our business and about how minority business development really works. Many things we already knew but were not using. For example, we all knew minority programs could NOT make us competitive. Minority programs give us access to business elements that can act as accelerants. Our job is to use the accelerants to get our business to the next level. (Take a look at the Access to Accelerant Tree. It was a helpful tool for creating our plan to leverage the value of whatever access we have.)

It is funny. When we started this business we resented the idea that we even needed a special program. But over time we became more and more dependent upon them. It is just how the system works if you let it.

I also have to admit our heads were not completely straight about our role. I think we started to believe all of this was about us. We started to read our own press. We got larger than most minority firms and we started to think that made us big. What we were was too big for our britches. We now understand our role as a supplier much better. We understand that this is about our customers and we are here to provide what they need to be competitive.

Lourdes, maybe most important we rediscovered the power of individual relationships. We were reminded about the role relationships played in our growth and development. We also got a chance to see what happens when you lack relationships. Relationships are critical, not just because of the support they can provide, but also because of the candid feedback these people are willing to give. There is nothing worse than being messed up and having no one willing to tell you. Without relationships we would have lost this entire account and maybe our company. Relationships matter most.

It has been a stressful and difficult set of lessons to learn and we had to pay a hefty price to learn them. My guess is we would not have changed anything until something like this happened. I am confident we are a better company because of it.

Let's stay connected and continue to share our experiences. I look forward to talking with you soon.

Fenton

Fenton read the email over and clicked send. He gathered his things and walked to the door. He turned and paused to look back at his office for a moment. Fenton smiled, turned off the lights and made his way to the car. He wanted to stop by the park to give Hugh an update before he went to the Chamber's Town Hall meeting.

CHAPTER
14

LOOKING UP

This time Fenton beat Hugh to the park bench. "Hello, Fenton," Hugh said as he took a seat next to him. "Well, how did it turn out?"

"About as good as we could expect. I just talked to Fernando Pena from Republic this afternoon. We lost the Florida region but retained the rest of the account," Fenton replied.

"Fernando, huh? You guys are talking now," Hugh said, making fun of Fenton.

"Very funny, Hugh. I've learned my lesson about that."

"Sounds like you've learned a lot of lessons, Fenton, and I can feel your passion over the last few weeks. But it worries me a bit," Hugh explained.

"Why would my passion worry you?" Fenton asked.

"It's not your passion but the cycle that concerns me," Hugh explained. "I've seen this moment with you and many others before. This is the same excitement, clarity and focus you had when you convinced the bank to give you another chance 10 years ago. And your business took off then just like it is going to take off now. But have you thought about how you're going to make sure you don't get back in this position again?"

"I guess I hadn't seen the cycle. You're right. I see it now," Fenton admitted.

"Do you remember how you felt about your business a little over a month ago?" Hugh asked.

"Yes, I didn't feel so good. The stuff was hitting the fan," Fenton replied.

"And how do you feel about the business now?" Hugh pressed.

"I feel pretty good."

"So what's the difference from a month ago to now?" Hugh asked. "None of your plans have actually shown any results. You've just started to work on them. You haven't grown the business or gotten new contracts. As a matter of fact, given some of your plans you will likely get smaller before you get larger. So why do you feel better now than a month ago?"

Fenton thought for a moment. He was sure he felt better but he had not thought about why.

"Well," Fenton said slowly searching for his answer. "There is an element of relief that we kept at least a portion of the Republic account. But I felt better about the business even before we got that news. You know, Hugh, I feel better because we know more about what we need to do. I feel better because we've been spending time *thinking about the business* and not just *working in the business*," Fenton explained. "It just provides a sense of confidence that we didn't have before."

"So you feel better about the business because you've been looking up from the day-to-day grind. But now what? Fenton, the real test of a strong organization is what they do when they're busy and when they're successful," Hugh said. "That is when their true tendencies come out. That's when you can really tell what they think is important."

Hugh paused for a moment and turned on the bench to face Fenton. "What happens when the crisis passes and you guys get busy again? What happens when your management team gets back to working on the next contract? How do you make sure you don't let this happen again? How do you sustain what you guys have done?" Hugh asked.

"Those are great questions because we know from our experience that we'll never see the *real* opportunities with our heads down. That's how the business got stuck in a bad groove and wasn't able to go to the next level."

"So what's the answer, Fenton?"

"Honestly, some of it is time and some of it's discipline," Fenton said. "The management team is very busy but most of us can find 5 – 10% more time especially if we can find a way to stop doing things that don't add value. We have to keep asking ourselves one of your favorite questions; *is this the best use of my time, right now?"* Fenton added.

Hugh smiled and nodded his head. They just sat on the park bench. Fenton was thinking.

After a few moments Hugh asked. "So what are you thinking?"

"I'm thinking that time is one thing but that won't be enough. We have to find a way to instill a disciplined process to make sure even when we are busy and when we are successful that we keep looking up. That means doing specific things at specific times in a specific way. We need to actually *plan* to make looking up a part of what we do as a normal course of business."

"Ok. Give me some examples of what you're thinking," Hugh requested.

"Well, for example, something as simple as a monthly industry article discussion. We could distribute an industry article among key staffers. Let's just say the fourth Thursday of every month the group meets for lunch to discuss the article and the potential impact or opportunity for our firm."

Hugh nodded. "I like it."

Fenton paused for a moment and continued. "We should probably have minimum requirements for continuing education for employees. The education could include conferences, a set of articles, or relevant books. We could make this a part of their development plan and their performance evaluation. That would integrate learning directly into our operation."

"That sounds like it might work," Hugh said content to just listen. Fenton was on a roll.

"We could have a quarterly roundtable discussion on critical issues related to the business," Fenton added. "Strategic questions like: What are the biggest trends affecting our business? What are the biggest challenges to our future success? What will our customers need in the next five years, 10 years, 20 years and beyond? What will they demand from us? How will we have to change?"

"I think you're getting it," Hugh said. "Remember, the world really doesn't care what you *know* unless it shows up in what you *do*," Hugh said. "That's the value of looking up. Making sure it shows up in what you do."

"Thanks, Hugh, for caring enough to help me through all of this."

"Fenton, it's a pleasure to be of service and you've done all of the work. I've just been listening to you," Hugh said as he pushed himself up from the park bench. "Keep me posted on how things are going, Fenton. You are on the brink of something very special."

Fenton looked up to say goodbye, but Hugh was already gone. He looked at his watch. It was time for the Town Hall meeting to begin. *A Town Hall meeting on minority business development,* he thought as he walked down the path to his car. *This should be interesting.*

I want to be clear.
I'm not blaming or excusing.
I'm explaining the current state.

CHAPTER
15

A CANDID
COMMUNITY
CONVERSATION

The town hall meeting was setup in casual interview style designed to replicate a living room. There were two large, high back upholstered chairs on stage. There was an end table between the chairs with a pitcher of ice water and two long stem glasses. The audience lights were dim and spotlights lit the stage. The moderator was Bob Stewart, the Chairman of the board of directors of the Chamber of Commerce and a local CEO. The guest was Maxwell Albert, an expert in minority business development. He was particularly known for his balanced approach, candid outlook and focus on sustainable strategies to grow minority firms. The meeting was just starting when Fenton arrived. He looked around the room quickly. *There have to be 500 people here*, he thought. Fenton eased his way past a few people and sat down near the back.

"Good evening," Bob said, seated in one of the chairs and reading from his notes. "I want to welcome everyone to tonight's Town Hall meeting discussing the topic of minority business development. I want to thank the Chamber for taking the lead in organizing this gathering, and Republic for their sponsorship."

The audience applauded. Bob paused, waiting for them to finish and then continued.

"Our community has struggled with the issue of minority business development. We have invested in a number of programs and initiatives. Our outcomes have been mixed. The reality is none of our activity has really changed the business landscape in this region. There is a mix of opinions, from people who think we do too much already, to those who believe the business community is not really committed to minority business growth. Tonight we have one of the foremost experts in minority business development."

Bob went on to read a prepared introduction of Max Albert.

"Max, this evening is designed to be a candid conversation," Bob said. "So I'm going to attempt to ask the kind of questions that are likely on many people's minds but are difficult to ask. Let's start with a question about the premise of minority business development. Why isn't it just like any other business development? Why do minority owned firms still need special assistance to grow?"

"Wow, no warm up for me, huh?" Max said, smiling broadly. The crowd laughed. "The problem can be summed up as a need to play catch-up. It took our nation generations to build the systems, mechanisms, relationship networks and culture that have become our current infrastructure of entrepreneurship. Our economic system evolved over the last 400 years into what it is today. Minorities, and primarily Blacks, were not involved in the ownership part of that evolution. So those who were included have a tremendous head start. Think about how much our economy has grown and prospered over that period of time. Think about the wealth that has been created and the complex business approaches that have developed. We live in an evolved economy that demands resources and partnerships to succeed. Minorities still need special programs because they generally lack the things we know they need to be successful in this evolved environment. Some non-minorities respond that it didn't happen for their families either. And that's true. It didn't happen for many families. But the difference is it wasn't systematically withheld either."

Max paused briefly and then continued. "I want to be clear. I'm not blaming or excusing. I'm explaining the current state.

"Max, do you think the idea of providing resources to help minority owned firms get to the next level, as you say, is running out of energy?"

"Is the idea of minority business development running out of energy?" Max repeated shifting his eyes upward looking for the right words. "I wouldn't say it's running out of energy, but it's surely in a transition."

"Max, I can tell you I'm in conversations with community and business leaders and they wonder what else they can do," Bob said. "They wonder if they're doing too much already. They wonder why the results aren't better. They know socially they have to do something but I think minority business development is in danger of not mattering as much as it used to."

"I agree we're at a crossroads," Max replied. "Partially because we've been at it for some time. Partially because our political climate has changed, and partially because people believe we haven't gotten great results from our efforts. I'm often just as critical. But to say we've not seen the results may be premature."

Max leaned back in his chair and continued.

"First, we have made progress. I could even argue significant progress. The question is how well should we be doing right now?" he continued. "What should the numbers be? How many? How large? We've been investing in minority business development for one generation and what we really want is for it to be fixed. It's a *convenient* expectation but I'm not sure it's rational. Look," Max said, leaning forward facing the crowd. "Most of our efforts have been social solutions and haven't had enough to do with business. We staffed, measured and funded minority business development efforts using the same model we used for out-of-poverty programs. Based on what we've been doing, maybe we're actually doing *better* than we should be. There is no model out there to benchmark against. No other country is ahead of us on this."

"You just mentioned that we've been at this for a generation and we started down this road over 40 years ago because it was the right social thing to do," Bob explained as he set up the next question. "Has that reason changed? In other words, why does minority business development matter at all?"

"There are a lot of reasons it matters. The most significant reason is because entrepreneurship is the only real way to create wealth. And until we diversify wealth, nothing is really going to change. Think about how communities fundamentally operate. How decisions are made; how politicians are elected; how causes are funded and how people are made to *feel* included. The minority middle class is growing significantly but most people of color report that their communities don't *feel* any different. It doesn't feel inclusive because it really isn't. At least not at all economic levels. But that is the challenge."

"So you're saying minority business development is important because it can create the diverse wealth that creates the real change in the community. It's tough to get people's hearts warmed about helping a few minorities get wealthy," Bob added.

"It doesn't just make a few minorities wealthy. It opens opportunity for everyone to reach their entrepreneurial potential at whatever level that is. The tide of inclusion lifts all boats but they have to be able to get their boat in the water. Honestly, Bob, I think there is still a real and present social aspect of our motivation for minority business development. The good news is that there is an ever increasing set of economic motivators too. The ultimate payoff of a successful base of minority owned firms is an inclusive community that has everyone engaged at all of the levels of the economic system. These are the communities that will be the most globally competitive. These are the communities that will be attractive to a diverse workforce, tourism, and all the things a community wants." Max said.

"Max, we've established that our results have, at best, been mixed. Why haven't we gotten better results?" Bob asked.

"Well, it depends on what you mean by results. The programs have done a good job of increasing minority business start-up activity. They have created an infrastructure designed to increase access to capital, access to markets and access to technical assistance. There is a real base of minority owned firms that have been founded and that have thrived. That likely would not have happened without the efforts of the last 40 years or so. Those are results."

"What about economic impact," Bob asked.

"If you are talking about results in economic impact, those results are more complex to evaluate but have been more limited. It's not because we don't want *it* to happen. We are often not sure what *it* is. As you said earlier it's a struggle to make our mission something people perceive as the creation of wealth for a small number of entrepreneurs. That's just tough to sell to the board of a philanthropic organization or a government entity. Most of these organizations have a moral mission to help the under privileged. A five million dollar business with a CEO who wears designer suits and sends her children to private schools doesn't appear to need much help."

"It has surely been a tough sell around here," Bob admitted.

"Bob, I understand how people feel but we use this approach to increase community capacity all the time. Investing in the growth and development of minority businesses is no different from a developer becoming wealthy from a riverfront development project that has significant public dollars involved. Or the owner of a professional sports franchise gaining wealth from a new sports venue built with tax payer dollars. Or a few technology entrepreneurs leveraging a community's focus on growing technology based firms. I do understand that philosophically it's tough, but the evidence is there. Think about it this way. When the community needs something they go to those relatively few who have the resources to make it happen. Those few get to decide what they will or won't do because it's their money. They decide based on their own set of beliefs, reasons, and motivations. The outcomes of this process are how a community really functions. Until it functions with diverse decisions, enabled by diverse *real* wealth, it can't be truly inclusive."

"I'm the chairman of the board of the Chamber of Commerce. We care about business growth and economic vitality. And we want it for all of our community. So what do we do about it? How do we do it right and get the community results that will make our region more competitive?"

"You treat it like you do other things that matter. You find strategies that will work given the specific make-up of your community. You commit the type of talent needed to drive results. You invest in that talent with the intensity of time needed to make an impact. You make it more and more about business outcomes and less and less about social indicators," Max explained leaning up in his seat and using his fingers to count.

"You increase your expectations for success and for everyone to play their role. There is a role in this for everyone. The community has a role. This forum is an example of that. The corporate community has a role to invest in business strategies that are inclusive. A local corporate leader like Republic is an example of that. And minority business owners have a role to leverage programs to get to the next level."

Max leaned back and reached for his glass of water. He sipped from it and continued to hold it in his hand.

"Max, we have just about a minute before we raise the lights and get the audience involved. We have been trying to get this right for more than 40 years," Bob explained. "Government programs, community based initiatives and corporate engagement. Are there any core basics or guiding principles you can leave us with?

"Well, there are five basic laws that form the foundation for getting to the next level: 1) Minority business growth will not happen naturally. 2) It has to be about business. 3) Access is like oxygen. You have to have it. 4) We can't let

Five Basic Laws

Basic law number one — It will NOT happen naturally. In many ways we have come a long way and we still have a way to go. Minority business growth and the inclusion of minority firms in the economic system will not happen without our overt attention to it.

Basic law number two — It has to be about business. I know we all say it but when we get down to it, we often make it about something else. There is a temptation to make it about things like poverty, low to moderate census tracks and even about a reduction in crime. All of those things are important and a thriving economy in which everyone is included will surely help. But those elements are complex, long-term social issues. We cannot burden minority firms with the weight of solving problems society has been unable to solve for hundreds of years.

Basic law three — Access is like oxygen. Access is imperative to sustain the life of a business but it is not enough to propel success. The access to market, access to capital and access to technical assistance models are the Sacred Trilogy of our approach to minority business development. These efforts are important but the presence of such programs does not equal success. Success in minority business development is a recipe of factors including the quality of the access programs, yet also including elements like the motivations of communities and major organizations, the expertise of the minority business owner, the quality of the business idea and so many more.

Basic law four — We cannot let race make us lose our common sense. Issues of race often make the smart people think in ways that are not so smart. Issues of race are so charged with emotion and even fear. There is a strong temptation to do things like keep programs that will never work, staff programs with people who do not have the right skills, measure success by means that do not matter. We would never think that way about anything that really mattered to our community, or our company. We can not think that way about minority business development.

Basic law five — There is a role for everyone to play. Where we are in this country on issues of race is no ones fault but everyone's opportunity. Major corporations, community leaders and minority business owners all have a critical role to play in getting to the next level.

race make us lose our common sense and 5) There is a role for everyone to play. Understand these and you have the basis to make real progress."

"Direct and to the point," Bob said as he turned to address the audience. "The five basic laws are explained in more detail in the handouts you received. Simple concepts but difficult to actually make happen," Bob said looking for Max's agreement.

"Yes, simple concepts. Complex reality," Max said.

The audience lights came up and Bob began to take questions for Max.

Fenton relaxed into his seat and smiled. He was thinking more than he was listening now. *Our community's approach to minority business development is not perfect,* he thought. *But the fact that we're talking candidly with each other is hopeful. There is a role for each of us and we all really want the same thing; thriving, competitive businesses as a base to a competitive community. Talking gives us a chance.*

And a real chance is all you can hope for. Everyone has to do everything they can to be ready to compete. That is the road to getting to the next level.

WHAT DO I DO NEXT?

Now what do you do? The short answer is, do something! Pull the big ideas from the book. Candidly review your own situation. What will it take for you and your organization to get to the next level? Consider which of the ideas matter most to you reaching your goals and objectives and start with them.

We have developed a web site to provide additional tools you can use to take some action right away. You will find assessment tools, checklists, planning tools and additional information. Visit the website at www.GetTheNextLevel.com.

The key message is that access is critical but not sufficient for our future success. Our focus has to be on our common commitment to be competitive. We have to get to the next level to find the real opportunities of inclusion.

ABOUT THE AUTHOR
MELVIN J. GRAVELY II, PH.D.

D r. Gravely is the founder of the *Institute for Entrepreneurial Thinking, Ltd.* a think tank whose mission is to improve the results of minority business development activities. He is an advisor to chambers of commerce, business support organizations, major corporations and minority businesses across the nation. He is a popular speaker and a noted thought leader in minority business development. Dr. Gravely is the editor of **The Entrepreneurial Thinker** newsletter and the author of five other books including the two others in this series **The Lost Art of Entrepreneurship** and **When Black and White Make Green**.

He has a BS in computer science from Mount Union College and an MBA from Kent State University. Dr. Gravely's Ph.D. is in Business Administration and Entrepreneurship from the Union Institute and University. He currently lives in Cincinnati with his family.

Your Feedback Please

If you enjoyed this book you will also like reading the previous two books in the series. In *The Lost Art of Entrepreneurship* and *When Black and White Make Green*, you will encounter many of the characters you enjoyed in this book, including wise old Hugh, Fenton, Carol and even Max Albert. The other two books are both powerful stories full of practical lessons and solid strategies. The reads are quick and entertaining and the proven approaches create lasting results.

We want to hear from you. What did you think of *Getting to the Next Level*? How did the book affect your business, supplier program or community efforts? Tell us about your success stories discussing and implementing the ideas.

You can email us at:
info@entrethinking.com

Or

Institute for Entrepreneurial Thinking, Ltd.
Attn: Getting to the Next Level
P.O. Box 621170
Cincinnati, OH 45262-1170

You can find the tools referenced in
Getting to the Next Level and more at
www.GetTheNextLevel.com